# Mandala Color Art

*Copyright: Published in the United States by Jimmy Mapes*
*Published January 2017*
*ISBN-13: 978-1542651950*
*ISBN-10: 1542651956*

# Thank you

www.ingramcontent.com/pod-product-compliance
Lightning Source LLC
Chambersburg PA
CBHW081555280526
45788CB00011B/3477